Tides Of Joy And Sorrow

Niharika Salian

BookLeaf
Publishing

India | USA | UK

Made with ❤ on the BookLeaf Publishing Platform
www.bookleafpub.in
www.bookleafpub.com

Dedication

To my mother and brother, for always standing by me, for always encouraging me to pursue my dreams and for never letting me give up.

Acknowledgement

I would like to thank my family and friends for inspiring me to write and also for being with me through both the good and bad times. To my mom for always being my rock and for encouraging me to pen my feelings down on paper. To my English teachers in school for helping me develop a strong command over the English language.

Preface

Ever since I started writing poems, it has always translated into me pouring my emotions onto paper. A piece of me always exists somewhere between the lines of my poems. I hope that my poems manage to reach out to you and that my emotions appeal to you. These poems talk about both joyful and sad things because as they say, happiness cannot exist without sadness and vice versa.

So let me take you on a journey, one poem at a time.

1. Above the clouds

Above the clouds I float
Feeling pure and so free
All I want to do is gloat
That no one can touch me
All the pain that lies below
Seems so distant and isolated
Peace within me seems to flow
And I feel constantly elated
I don't want to touch down
I fear what awaits me
On my face will appear a frown
And tears will flow freely
This seems a happy place
With nature around me
The air around me is scarce
But at least no one can hurt me

2. World of Fiction

When I open a book
I forget about reality
I just sit in a nook
And forget about cruelty
The world of fiction
Calls to me always
It's a good addiction
Helps me pass my days
Sometimes I feel like
Entering that fantasy land
I wish I could take a hike
But all are clutching my hand
That world seems peaceful
Far from the harsh reality
But how I long to be blissful

When I'm bound by this duality
Will someone let me fly
And reach the stars
Or will I finally die
And then be rid of my scars

3. By The Water Tank

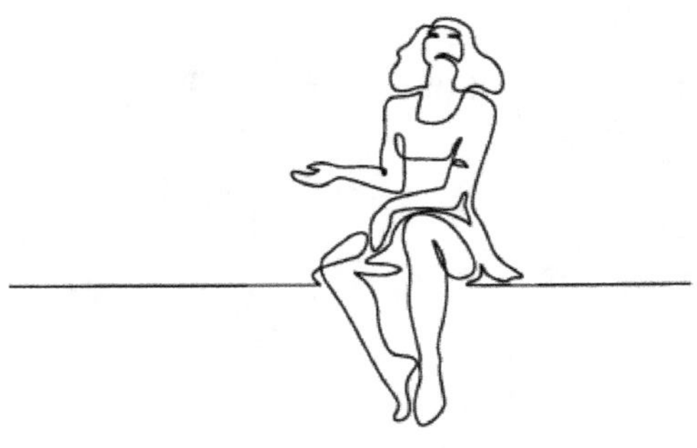

She went there for the solitude
For the peace and quiet in the air
This was all part of her fortitude
As the wind blew in her hair
She wondered about life
She wondered about pain
If she ever was to be a wife
Or if there was nothing to gain
The world was a bitter place
But she held her ground
She owned her own lovely space
And embraced the self-love she had found
She knew love was a bittersweet thing
It could stab you in the heart
Or it could make you sing

So, she had no choice but to restart
As the birds swirled above her head
She vowed to always be strong
She vowed till the day she was dead
She would always sing her own song

4. My Love for Travel

I love to travel and explore the world
The places I see fill me with glee
Into the plane I wish to be hurled
And go to all the places I wish to see
Travel opens our minds and hearts
Makes us open to different cultures
As each new adventure starts
I look forward to all the novel ventures
How I wish to disappear somewhere
And stay away from this boring life
At each place I breathe in the air
I wish to forget all this inane strife
Take me somewhere I can be lost
To a place where I can be truly free
I wish to do this soon at any cost
For this is what fills me with glee

5. My Mother

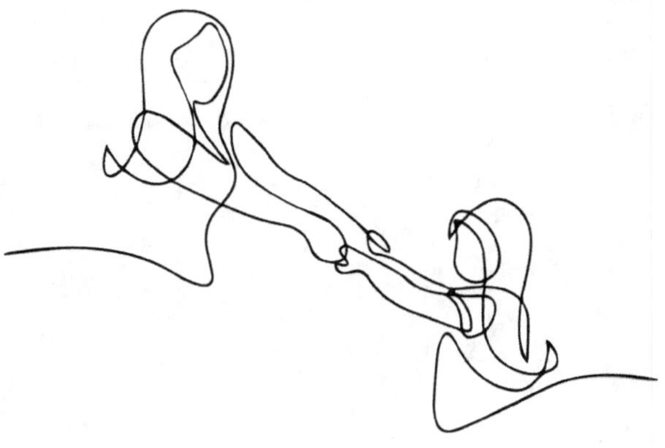

She wipes so many of our tears away
Tries to make sure they don't recur
As babies, with us she would play
Those years have gone by in a blur
She has been my biggest strength
My rock when I needed her support
I don't know how to thank her at length
So that's why to these words I resort
Thank you, my dearest mother,
For doing so much for our family
I could never ask for any other
You're the best mom in the galaxy!
I know you have gone through a lot

Still, you have remained strong throughout
Making things right I know I cannot
But for you, I will always be on the lookout

6. Mother Earth

With these trees falling around me
I begin to realize nature's anger
Maybe we should just let everything be
And save Mother Earth while we're still eager
The winds howling and pulling down trees
Is nature's way of telling us to stop
I truly wish that mankind sees
What a huge mess we have to mop
It's never too late to respect nature again
And to mend all our constant misdeeds
Let's remove all of Mother Earth's pain
And make sure we sow some more seeds
I make this humble appeal to humankind
To stop taking Mother Earth for granted
Let each one of us make up our mind
To repair whatever evil we have started

7. Depression

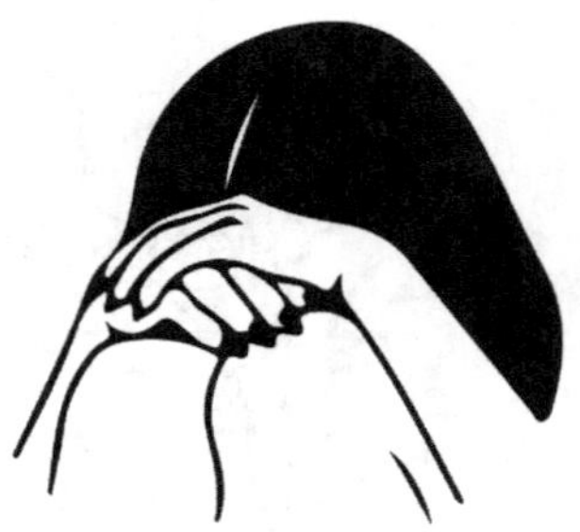

How do I get out of this depression?
It refuses to let go of me completely
It continues to have me in its possession
And I try to fight against it weakly
As it tightens its grip around my mind
I struggle to find my way in the world
I feel as if I am slowly becoming blind
And another me has somehow emerged
I must make sure it doesn't win at all
I must fight with all I have within me
I must ignore it when to me it will call
I have to find a way to set myself free
Who knows if it returns to me again?
Will I fight or succumb to it once more?
I must deal with all this numbing pain
And return to the way things were before

8. What is Love?

"What is love?" is often asked
To those who believe in it
In love who all have basked
Will offer their advice a bit
Love is a wonderful thing
Some will say wistfully
It makes our hearts sing
As we dance blissfully
Others say that love hurts
It causes so much pain
Maybe your heart bursts
If you love someone in vain
I say love is needed in this world

To remind us we need each other
In love we need to be whirled
It doesn't matter who is your lover
Let's learn to love again once more
Let's lose ourselves in one another
There's something worth fighting for
Since love is indeed a beautiful color

9. Loneliness

Every night as I lie down in my bed
This wave of loneliness engulfs me
I feel so sad and a sense of dread
Takes over and sleep isn't an actuality
Why do I have no one to call my own?
Friends exist but have their own life
In this world I feel I am all alone
Every day I must deal with this strife
I have this innate fear in my mind
That I will eventually die alone
A trustworthy friend I need to find
Before my heart turns to stone

10. Highs and Lows

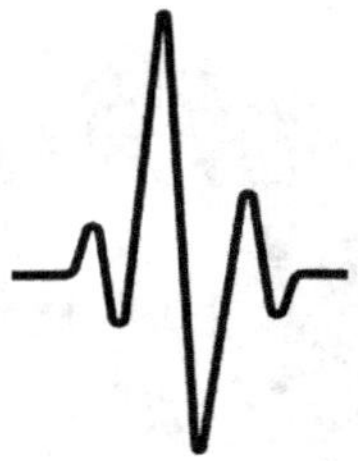

Sometimes I feel so low
Sometimes I'm ecstatic
Either life becomes slow
Or sometimes it gets manic
I feel stuck in my life
Like there's no way out
Why do I face such strife?
I want to scream and shout
I know I need to recover
Bounce back to who I was
I have with me the power
To reach for the stars
But I know I'll be fine
And find the silver lining
Take back what's mine
And come out shining

11. Numbness

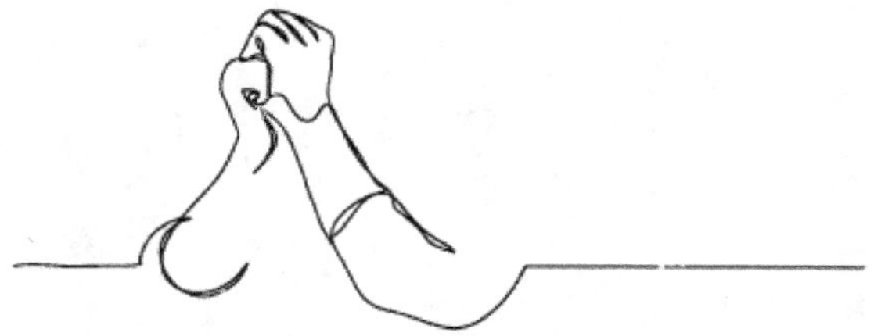

Why do I feel so numb?
No anger or pain
Maybe I'm just dumb
Or unable to take this strain
It takes so much effort
To get out of my bed
I need a sense of comfort
Before I bang my head
It's easy for you to say
Get up and do something
But nothing seems okay
I can't get past this feeling
My only hope is a miracle
A tiny ray of sunshine
Maybe then I'll go and tackle
And grab what's truly mine

12. Giving Up

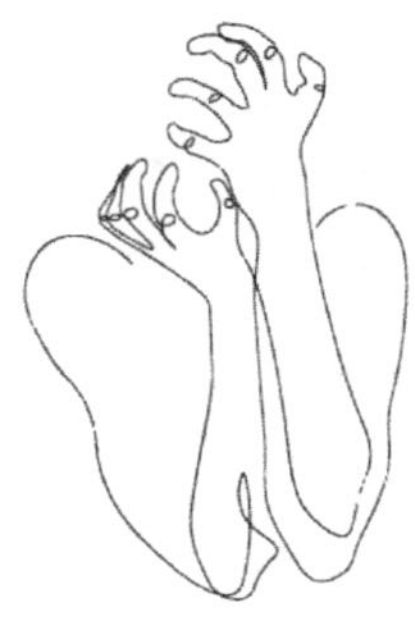

Sometimes I feel like giving up
The pressure feels too much
These feelings that I develop
Are what I want to clutch
Why do people behave like this
Push us past a breaking point
My days of yonder I do miss
Now I can't help but be paranoid
I need to make myself stronger
I need to make myself see
But at times I seriously wonder
Is this who I want to be?
Giving up is not at all an option
I need to move along a free bird
Need to find my inner passion
Even if people find me a bit weird

13. Therapy

What she writes on her paper
Makes me really wonder
As my sweat turns into vapor
I'm taken back to the days of yonder
It hurts to relive my memories
And to go back into the past
Yet she offers many remedies
That won't make the pain last
I have nothing against anyone
But I need to feel much better
As all my sessions get done
I'm definitely going to thank her
It's not easy to open up to her
It definitely takes a lot of guts
But as the days pass by in a blur
She will make sure I don't go nuts!

14. My Brother

He arrived 8 years after me
In his eyes, wisdom I can see
Practical and sensible he is
Unlike his unpredictable sis
Although he is way younger
Age is just another number
I go to him for some advice
He also happens to be so nice
I will always be protective of him
Especially when matters are grim
The true bond of being a sibling
Started way back in the beginning
I wish nothing but the best for you

I pray all your dreams come true
You're one of the best souls I know
And to you, everything I owe

15. The Virus

Oh, what a dreadful world we live in
Someone lives and someone dies
As you end up losing a next of kin
What echoes is the pain-filled cries
The virus has a mind of its own
It doesn't see color, creed or class
So many families apart it has torn
Others have been given a free pass
I truly wish for mankind to unite
And not to make another mistake
By common sense let us fight
As we know our lives are at stake

16. Music

Music fills me with so much joy
It transports me to another world
It's the only thing I really enjoy
My mind remains truly preserved
As the notes flow into my ear
This calmness descends upon me
I feel there is nothing I need to fear
I feel like flying high because I'm free
I've been gifted with this talent
Of playing music, and singing too
As I play, I become very silent
And the tears become very few
I wish to sing to the whole world
The stories of my joy and pain
And as all my songs are heard
I will be free to sing again and again

17. Caged Lioness

Why don't you understand
What I'm going through
I try and raise my hand
But it doesn't reach you
I know I'm a useless rebel
But I have lost my voice
I'm at the highest decibel
But it's just white noise
I'm like a caged lioness
Fighting to break finally free
But this world is a mess
And I have lost the real me
My pleas fall on deaf ears
Everyone tries and subdues me
But no one sees my tears
So now it's time for me to flee

18. Joy

Joy may be just a small three-letter word
But it can forever change someone's world
Joy can be different for every single person
That is why everyone has a different version
For some, it means amassing tremendous
wealth
For others, it simply means having great
health
For me, joy means enjoying each day as it
comes
Living each day without worrying about the
outcomes
Music, movies, fashion, travel give me so
much joy
I hate it when my joy someone tries to
destroy

It's difficult for me to always see the bright
side
But at least I can say to myself that I
somehow tried
Joy is something I try to feel every single day
Though my true feelings are at times hard to
say
I wish that joy becomes a constant part of me
Out of the darkness, I wish the light to see

19. My Warrior King

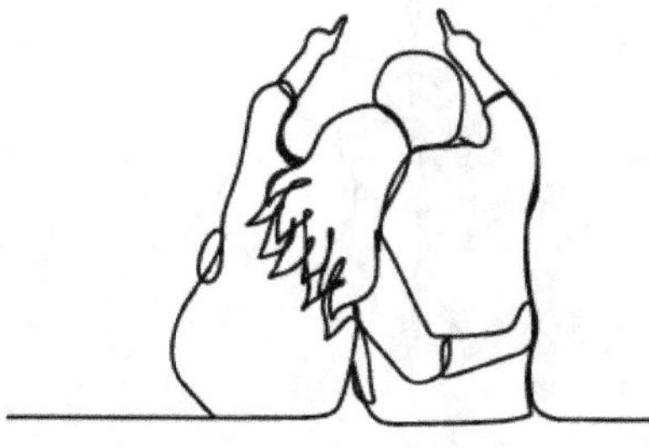

He entered my life like a hurricane
He filled it with laughter and joy
I had nothing to lose or to gain
But he wasn't just any other boy
He made me believe in love again
Calmed my nerves when I was rattled
Made me forget all my internal pain
All the demons I had in my life battled
He may not be completely perfect
But he is mine, as I remind everyone
I value the most our strong connect
It cannot be destroyed by anyone
He is absolutely my warrior king
Riding away into the lovely sunset
My ultimate joy only he can bring
As our love is imperfectly perfect

20. Dreamcatcher

When you do dream so badly at night
Things that give you a tremendous fright
The dream catcher hangs over your bed
Giving you some relief from your dread
It is smartly designed like a spider's web
And all your bad dreams it will forever ebb
I hang mine over me all through the night
Making sure I wake up fresh and bright
The various colors of it catch your eyes
Hanging it over your bed would be wise
I've had mine above for so many years
It has completely allayed all of my fears
So let us forget about all our nightmares
The bad dreams that give us the jitters
Let's wake up extremely fresh every day
And pray for bad dreams to stay away

21. Warrior Queen

She chose to go through life alone
Like a single brave warrior queen
It was like stepping into the unknown
But this was soon to be a routine
She had dealt with a lot in her past
It continued to haunt her in the present
The pain seemed to endlessly last
And it was oh so very unpleasant
With the help of family and friends
She killed her problems one by one
Her troubles that seemed immense
Slowly, steadily dwindled to none
As she gradually held her head up high
She began to realize the truths of life
She looked up at the great blue sky
And realized she had to deal with her strife